Supersize Animals

By Melvin and Gilda Berger

Scholastic Inc.

Think of people you know. Some are short, some are tall. Everyone is a little different. The same is true for animals. Each species has animals of all sizes, from small to large. But did you know that certain animals grow much, MUCH larger than all others of their kind? They are the Supersize Animals!

Great Dane

When a Great Dane stands on all four legs, it is almost twice as tall as most other dogs. But watch out when it gets up on its **hind legs**. Then, it can reach higher than the top of a grown-up's head! A Great Dane named Zeus holds the title of Tallest Dog Ever.

Savannah Cat

House cats are closely related to big African wildcats. Over the years, people **mated** house cats with wildcats to make a new breed of house cat called the Savannah. Paw to shoulder, Savannahs are more than twice as tall as common house cats. The tallest house cat, named Trouble, is in the *Guinness Book of World Records*.

Japanese Spider Crab

Did you ever hear of a crab as big as a car? If not, meet the giant Japanese spider crab. The spider crab can sit on a car's roof—and its 10 legs will hang down to the ground! It lives in the Pacific Ocean, near Japan. For a very good reason, the Japanese call this huge creature *taka-ashi-gani,* which means "tall-legs crab."

Giant Snail

Most snails that live on land are quite small. But some grow to be supersize and set records. The biggest snail was found in Africa in 1976. It was named Gee Geronimo like the famous Native American Apache warrior. Although Gee Geronimo comes from Africa, giant land snails live all over the world.

Leatherback Turtle

A turtle that lives in the sea, the leatherback is the largest of all turtles. It is the only turtle with a flat, leathery back instead of a hard, bony shell. The longest leatherback on record washed ashore in 1988. It was half the length of a pickup truck!

Goliath Bird-eater

Of all the spiders in the world, the biggest is the goliath bird-eater. Its body, including its 8 legs, is as big as a full-size dinner plate! But despite its name, the goliath bird-eater spider eats few birds. It sometimes grabs a small, sleeping bird before it can fly away. But it mainly feeds on insects.

Continental Giant Rabbit

Almost everyone thinks that rabbits are small, furry animals with long ears and short, fluffy tails. But did you know that some rabbits grow to be almost as long as broom handles? Darius holds the title of the world's longest rabbit. This huge bunny eats 12 carrots, 2 apples, and 1/2 a cabbage every single day!

Goldfish

Goldfish are the most popular pet fish. Most live in tanks where they are fed by hand and stay small. Others are kept in warm ponds or lakes. Here they find lots of food to eat. These outdoor goldfish can grow to be supersize! The record setter, discovered in Holland, was the length of a large newborn baby!

Flying Fox Bat

The flying fox bat is a supersize member of the bat family. With its wings spread out, the flying fox bat is as big as a large goose! Most other bats have a **wingspan** closer to that of a robin. The flying fox bat is also known for its fox-like face. But it's not a **carnivore** like a fox. It mostly feeds on fruit—and never harms animals or people.

Whale Shark

The whale shark is the biggest fish in the sea. Yet it feeds only on the smallest plants and animals it finds in the water! This shark swims along with its huge mouth open, swallowing anything that floats inside. The biggest whale shark on record is about the size of a *Tyrannosaurus rex*!

Belgian
Horse

Long ago, knights in heavy armor used big, strong horses to carry them into battle. From these horses came the Belgian horses, which are among the tallest of today's horses. You may have seen Big Jake, the modern record holder who helps pull show wagons in parades. He is named for the star of the movie *Big Jake*.

Python Snake

Python snakes live near small rivers or ponds in tropical Asian rain forests. The longest snake of all time was a python from the 1900s. It was about as long as a large school bus! Giant pythons are so long and heavy that it takes 9 strong people to hold a live one!

Lion's Mane Jellyfish

The record-holding lion's mane jellyfish washed up on a beach in 1870. Its string-like **tentacles** were about half the length of a football field. That is almost 1,000 times the length of the tentacles of an average jellyfish! The lion's mane jellyfish is actually one of the longest animals in the world!

Goliath Frog

The goliath frog was named for the biblical warrior Goliath, who was said to be almost twice the size of other soldiers. Indeed, goliath frogs are about twice as long as most other frogs. In fact, they are the largest frogs in the whole world! Although small at birth, they grow to be longer than most cats!

Glossary

Carnivore - An animal that eats meat

Hind legs - The back or rear legs of an animal

Mate - To join together to produce babies

Tentacle - One of the long, flexible limbs of some animals, such as the octopus and squid

Wingspan - The distance between one end of a bird's wing and the other